Journey

Fruit of the Spirit Series - PATIENCE

(Black & White Pages)

A Journey worth journaling your way through...
Your LIFE!

Write the Vision... Dream!

Make it Plain... Plan.

You Got this! ... Take action!!

Your Focus for this Journal!

DEDICATION:

Dedicated to my Savior Jesus who has given me a peace that is beyond measure! His LOVE for me has been a guiding rock that has allowed me to face this world with PATIENCE in all areas of my life!

To my beloved Robin whom I have watched faced the daily battle with long-suffering galore! Who has supported me in all things, I dedicate this to your faithfulness to stay in a state of PATIENCE that it beyond limits!!
I love you Robin aka Mr. Miller!
Cyndilu

Copyright © 2020 by Cyndilu Miller and beBOLDyou™ Publishing

Cover Design: Cyndilu Miller

All Rights Reserved.

No part of this publication may be reproduced, distributed, or transmitted in any form or by any means, including photocopying, recording, electronic or mechanical methods, or by any information storage and retrieval system, without the prior written permission of the publisher and author, except the case of brief quotations embodied in critical reviews and certain other non-commercial uses permitted by copyright law.

ISBN: 9798569407217 - Black & White Version
Independently published:
beBOLDyou™ Publishing
10 Bell Street
Owaka 9535
New Zealand

Website:
www.beboldyou.com
Email:
beboldyou@gmail.com

QUOTE of the Day

A person's wisdom
yields patience;
it is to one's glory to
overlook an offense.

Proverbs 19:11

QUOTE of the Day

Patience beyond measure is a gift that I give others when I live it!

~Cyndilu Miller

Journey Journals - *Patience*

QUOTE of the Day

Through patience a ruler can
be persuaded, and a
gentle tongue can break a bone.

Proverbs 25:15

Journey Journals - *Patience*

QUOTE of the Day

Silence is not only golden it is the key to living a life of patience with unconditional love.

~Cyndilu Miller

Journey Journals - *Patience*

QUOTE of the Day

The end of a matter is better than its beginning, and patience is better than pride.

Ecclesiastes 7:8

Journey Journals - *Patience*

QUOTE of the Day

Let not our own desire to push ahead be the undoing of our patience but rather the fuel for long-suffering indeed!

~Cyndilu Miller

Journey Journals - *Patience*

QUOTE of the Day

...being strengthened with all power according to his glorious might so that you may have great endurance and patience...

Colossians 1:11

Journey Journals - *Patience*

QUOTE of the Day

May the gift of patience carry me through all things, may it be the gift that speaks volumes to all those watching my life along the way!

~Cyndilu Miller

Journey Journals - *Patience*

QUOTE of the Day

Therefore, as God's chosen people, holy and dearly loved, clothe yourselves with compassion, kindness, humility, gentleness and patience.

Colossians 3:12

Journey Journals - *Patience*

QUOTE of the Day

Patience is easier when we live from a place of knowing no matter what it will be well with my soul!

~Cyndilu Miller

Journey Journals - *Patience*

QUOTE of the Day

Preach the word; be prepared in season and out of season; correct, rebuke and encourage—with great patience and careful instruction.

1 Timothy 4:2

Journey Journals - *Patience*

QUOTE of the Day

Patience that comes from our minds can not carry us where patience pouring out of love will!

~Cyndilu Miller

Journey Journals - *Patience*

QUOTE of the Day

We do not want you to become lazy,
but to imitate those who through faith and
patience inherit what has been promised.

Hebrews 6:12

Journey Journals - *Patience*

QUOTE of the Day

One knows one is full of patience when life is throwing curve balls and still there is a knowing that all things will become straight in due time!

~Cyndilu Miller

Journey Journals - *Patience*

QUOTE of the Day

Be patient, then, brothers and sisters, until the Lord's coming. See how the farmer waits for the land to yield its valuable crop, patiently waiting for the autumn and spring rains.

James 5:7

Journey Journals - *Patience*

QUOTE of the Day

When my heart is focused on patience it grows a garden of thanksgiving in the storm!

~Cyndilu Miller

Journey Journals - *Patience*

QUOTE of the Day

You too, be patient and stand firm, because the Lord's coming is near.

James 5:8

beBOLDyou™
Journey Journals - *Patience*

QUOTE of the Day

Gratitude is one of the quickest ways to shift your heart stance to patience through all things!

~Cyndilu Miller

Journey Journals - *Patience*

_____

_____

_____

_____

_____

_____

_____

_____

_____

_____

_____

_____

QUOTE of the Day

Bear in mind that our Lord's patience means salvation, just as our dear brother Paul also wrote you with the wisdom that God gave him.

Isaiah 26:3

Journey Journals - *Patience*

QUOTE of the Day

Patience is like an umbrella to my soul...with the ability to withstand the storms and not get soaked.

~Cyndilu Miller

beBOLDyou™
Journey Journals - *Patience*

QUOTE of the Day

Be still before the Lord and wait patiently for him; do not fret when people succeed in their ways, when they carry out their wicked schemes.

Psalm 37:7

Journey Journals - *Patience*

QUOTE of the Day

When we let go of our need for it all to be perfect for patience we can see the beauty in the progress and growth!

~Cyndilu Miller

QUOTE of the Day

I waited patiently for the Lord;
he turned to me and heard my cry.

Psalm 40:1

Journey Journals - *Patience*

QUOTE of the Day

When we trust that God has
our greatest good in mind for us
we find a strength to waiting patiently!

~Cyndilu Miller

QUOTE of the Day

Whoever is patient has
great understanding,
but one who is
quick-tempered displays folly.

Proverbs 14:29

Journey Journals - *Patience*

QUOTE of the Day

When we seek patience with all men we find peace with their ways and contentedness in our own selves too!

~Cyndilu Miller

beBOLDyou™
Journey Journals - *Patience*

QUOTE of the Day

A hot-tempered person stirs up conflict,
but the one who is patient calms a quarrel.

Psalm 4:8

Journey Journals - *Patience*

QUOTE of the Day

Stay ever focused on the Lord and living from a place of patience will become a part of your daily routine!

~Cyndilu Miller

beBOLDyou™
Journey Journals - *Patience*

QUOTE of the Day

Be completely humble and
gentle; be patient,
bearing with one another in love.

Ephesians 4:2

beBOLDyou™
Journey Journals - Patience

QUOTE of the Day

Patience comes as we relinquish our expectations and replace them with the hope and knowing that all things work together for good!

~Cyndilu Miller

Journey Journals - *Patience*

QUOTE of the Day

Love is patient, love is kind.
It does not envy, it does not boast,
it is not proud.

1 Corinthians 13:4

You can find more Journey Journals on Amazon -
Look Up Author Cyndilu Miller

Cyndilu is the founder of the beBOLDyou Personality Expressions System™
That will help you with re-framing the stories you tell yourself every day that
direct and guide your life even when you are not aware it is happening.

One of the things we need to do is to re-frame our thoughts and thinking on
the Fruits of the Spirit is just one way we can do that.
Enjoy this series.

You can connect with Cyndilu here:
on Facebook - www.facebook.com/beboldyou
on Instagram - www.instagram.com/beboldyouwithcyndilu
on Pinterest - www.Pinterest.com/beboldyou

You can also find the Great Interview Series on the beBOLDyou™ Podcast
with Cyndilu which is available on many platforms including Apple iTunes®,
Spotify®, and Google Play® to name just a few.

Printed in Great Britain
by Amazon